GOD MADE Activity Book

Science activities celebrating God's creation

Illustrated by Steph Marshall

lion cub books

This edition copyright © 2024 Lion Hudson IP Limited
Text by Deborah Lock
Illustrated by Steph Marshall
Consultants Steph Bryant and Lizzie Henderson

Published by **Lion Cub Books**
Part of the SPCK Group
SPCK Group, Studio 101, The Record Hall, 16–16A Baldwin's Gardens, London EC1N 7RJ, UK
spckpublishing.co.uk

ISBN 978-1-915748-09-6

First edition 2024

10 9 8 7 6 5 4 3 2 1

Acknowledgments
All illustrations by Steph Marshall, except: pp. 2, 3, 11 cloud © Getty Images/Ihor Biliavskyi;
pp. 5, 6, 7 space background © Getty Images/kbeis; pp. 5, 6, 7 shooting stars © Getty
Images/kbeis; p. 6 speech bubble © Getty Images/Pikusisi-Studio; p. 21 grey bin © Getty
Images/Anna Bielousova; p. 21 green recycling bin © Getty Images/agungsptr; pp. 12,
18, 20 notebook © Getty Images/yugoro; pp. 14, 15, 18, 19, 20, 21 blades of grass © Getty
Images/higyou.
A catalogue record for this book is available from the British Library
Printed and bound in China by Dream Colour (Hong Kong) Printing Ltd

Produced on paper from sustainable sources

Contents

Look far away

What can you see in the night sky?

Go outside on a clear night. Draw the moon and any stars you can see.

God made space. He made everything that has ever existed in the whole universe. He made the huge rocky asteroids and icy comets that zoom around. And he made the stars that sparkle and shine because they are very, very hot.

What shape does the moon look like in your picture?
Tick the shape you can see.

new ⬜

crescent  ⬜

half ⬜

full  ⬜

Look up

Where does the light come from during the day?

Put the planet stickers in the right place.

Hint: Match the stickers to their size.

MERCURY

EARTH

VENUS

SUN

MARS

Can you?

- Find the largest planet.

- Find the smallest planet.

- Find the planet we live on.
  Hint: it has plant-covered land and a watery sea.

- Find the planet that has the longest year.
  Hint: it is furthest from the Sun.

- Find the planet that has the shortest year.
  Hint: it is closest to the Sun.

A year on a planet is the length of time it takes to spin around the Sun.

God made the planets. Planets spin around stars. Our world, named "Earth", is one of the planets that spin around a star we call the Sun. Even though it is far away, the Sun is so hot and bright that it gives us light and warmth.

JUPITER

NEVER LOOK STRAIGHT AT THE SUN!

URANUS

SATURN

NEPTUNE

Look down

What is our world made of?

Our world is covered with rocky land and water.
Draw a snow-capped mountain, a river, and a forest to
complete this picture.

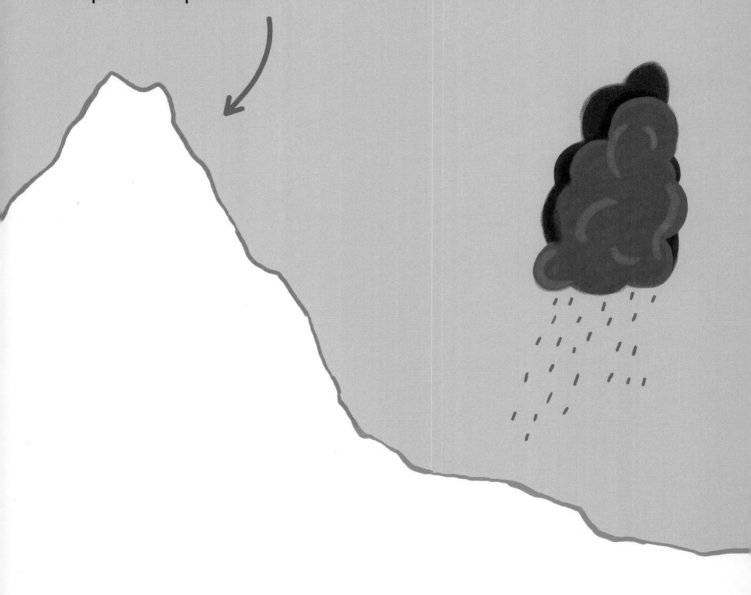

Are there any rivers, forests, or
mountains near to where you live?

God made the world. Our world is mostly made of rock and metals. The rock is cold and hard on the surface, making the ground we walk on. This is called the crust. Under the crust, the rock is very hot and sticky.

In special places, the hot, sticky rock shoots up from under the Earth's crust. We call these volcanoes.
Follow the code to complete the picture of inside a volcano.

1 Red – hot sticky rock under the surface

2 Orange – hot sticky rock on the surface

3 Brown – layers of the Earth's crust

Look outside

What is the weather like outside?

Make a weather chart for the week.
You can use these shapes to show the weather or draw your own.

Sunny

Cloudy

Rainy

Windy

Snowy

	Monday	Tuesday	Wednesda
Morning			
Afternoon			

God made water. Every day, water from puddles, lakes, and oceans gets warmed by the Sun and floats up into the sky to make clouds. Clouds can be blown a long way before they drop the water again as rain or snow.

Tick the shapes and sizes of the clouds you see this week.
You can tick more than one.

Small and wispy   ☐

Big and fluffy   ☐

Huge and stormy   ☐

Thursday	Friday	Saturday	Sunday

Look around

What sort of plants grow near you?

Go for a nature walk and look around for these things.

Tick what you find.

A tall tree

A pink flower

A small leaf

A short tree

A yellow flower

A large leaf

God made plants. When he was first making the world, water helped new living things to grow. Over time, plants and other living things grew in the oceans and then all over the land. Today, plants grow almost everywhere!

Collect some fallen leaves with different shapes and draw around them. Look to see how they are the same and how they are different.

Look back

What sort of animals lived a long time ago?

Use the stickers to match the shape of these animals that lived long before us. Which ones fly, which ones walk on land, and which ones swim?

God made animals. He made every animal that has ever lived. Over millions of years, the world has been filled with all kinds of wonderful animals. Fossils can help us learn about the animals that lived a long time ago. Today's animals are the great, great, great . . . grandchildren of some of these long ago animals!

Look at them

Why are animals different?

Match the animal to where it lives. Find these animal stickers and put them in the right habitat (place).

Polar Bear  Camel Whale

Can you?

- Find the animal with the thickest fur.

- Find the animal with a hump.

- Find the animal with strong flippers.

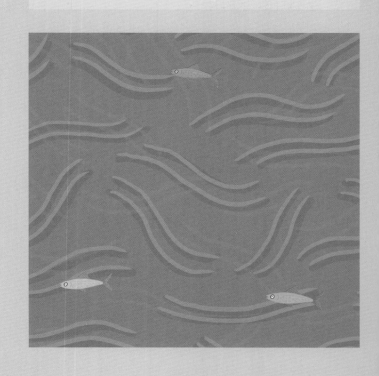

Different types of animals can look amazingly different from each other. They are all sorts of shapes and sizes with different patterns and markings. These differences can help animals to be good at different things and to live in different habitats all over the world.

Use the bird stickers to match the shape of these birds.

How are these birds different from each other?

- Look at their beaks.

- Look at their wings.

- Look at their feathers.

How do you think these differences help them to eat and do different things.

Look closer

GET AN ADULT TO HELP YOU LOOK UNDER ANYTHING HEAVY!

Where can you find the tiniest animals?

Go on a search for minibeasts. Take a look on the ground and on some leaves, or under rocks and logs. Use a magnifying glass for a closer look.

Tick what you see.

A butterfly ☐

A beetle ☐

A centipede ☐

An ant ☐

Look closely at each minibeast you find.

Does it have 0, 6, 8, or more legs?

Does it have wings so it can fly?

Does it have a pattern?

There are always new animals to discover, and even the smallest of them are special to God. God loves us to learn about his wonderful animals: where they live, what they can do, and how to look after them.

Draw your best minibeast inside the magnifying glass.

Look after

USE GLOVES AND WASH HANDS AFTERWARDS!

How can we take care of what God made?

Here are some ways to try and care for the world.

Tick what you can do.

- Spend time exploring nature. ☐

- Sort out paper, plastic, and cans, so that they can be recycled. ☐

- Reuse and refill a water bottle. ☐

- Put your wrappers in a bin. ☐

- Go on a litter-picking hunt. ⚠ ☐

- Save cardboard and plastic to reuse them for crafts. ☐

- Put fruit and vegetable peelings into the compost. ⚠ ☐

- Plant fruit and vegetable seeds and look after the plants as they grow. ☐

God made each of us and we are each good at different things. God asks us to love and look after everything that he made. We can all help to keep our world clean and healthy in different ways.

Follow the lines to find out who is not recycling.

Look forward

What would you like to do in the future?

What are these people doing? Use the stickers to complete each picture to find out.

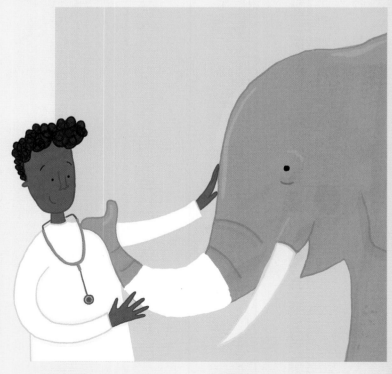

Can you?

- Find the vet, who is looking after animals.

- Find the astronaut, who is exploring space.

- Find the scientist, who is studying tiny things.

God has made each of us to be curious and creative. We have so many questions about the amazing universe God has made. To help us learn more, people have invented things like rockets, robots, microscopes, and telescopes.

Match the sticker to the topics. Of all the things that God has made, what would you like to find out more about? Tick the boxes and ask an adult to help you find out more.

Stars

Volcanoes

Animals

Planets

Weather

Plants

Find out more about the clues God has given us to learn how he made:

space,   the world,   and animals.

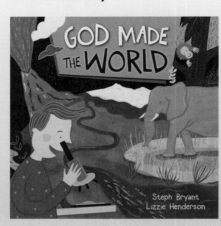
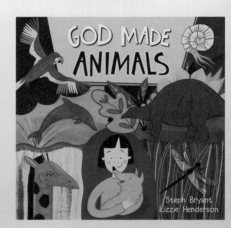

ISBN 9780745977836   ISBN 9780745977843   ISBN 9780745977850

More activities can be found at the back of these books, too.

www.faradaykids.com

The "God Made" series was produced in collaboration with the Faraday Institute for Science and Religion. The Faraday Institute is an interdisciplinary research and communication enterprise linked to the University of Cambridge. The Youth and Schools Team are committed to providing high-quality events and resources that encourage young people of all ages and backgrounds to explore their questions about the interactions of science and religious faith in exciting and engaging ways.

Why not explore more about science, faith, and what God has made at **www.faradaykids.com**. You'll find activities, videos, age-specific answers to common questions, and more about other resources. Or check out **www.faradayeducators.com** for information about resources and events for parents, teachers, and other educators.

This project and publication was made possible through the support of a grant from the John Templeton Foundation. The opinions expressed in this publication are those of the authors and do not necessarily reflect the views of the John Templeton Foundation.